Belteshazzar & Abednego

G000025561

The Mosque and Its Role in Society

Acknowledgements

The authors wish to express their genuine gratitude to all those who contributed in making this booklet a reality.

There are those who have read and critiqued, others helped in editing, and some with their artistic abilities, many with their encouragement and prayers. To all of them, we say a special 'thank you'. To all the friends who have helped in word or deed: your contributions have enriched this humble effort.

The authors

Contents

Preface

This is an in-depth report on a single word: mosque, a word which represents an institution increasingly in the news, and which is currently seen from a Western perspective as being in the mould of a church or temple—a place of worship—although in recent years, weapons and literature promoting terrorism have been found in key mosques in the U.K. and in Europe. These findings have raised an important question, or rather a set of questions which this report purports to address. They include: "Is a mosque just a place of worship? And, if so, what constitutes worship in Islam, such that it might include the sorts of military activities which have been found to be going on within its walls? And more importantly, why has there not been an outcry by Islamic authorities if these activities are really not sanctioned by Islam? There have been apologies and explanations by various authorities, but these protestations of innocence in regard to intent really have no teeth to prevent a repeat of the same. If they are serious, why not issue a fatwa, or judicial ruling to put a complete and final stop to this involvement within the mosques?

These are but a few of the key questions which provided the climate, background, and need for such a study as these authors have undertaken.

However, there is an even more dramatic reason for this study—the trigger being the clear and present danger represented by the announcement of a planned mega-mosque which would hold some 70,000 worshippers in Newham, East London, to be completed by the 2012 Summer Olympic Games. The current residents living in the affected community are understandably alarmed, and they want answers to these questions—and they want these answers now while there is time to make a reasoned assessment.

The authors, who, in making their free choice to leave Islam, are well qualified to speak on the need for guarding the freedoms of choice that we have in non-Islamic countries, and the long-range impact that this new mosque (or any mosque) has on any community—much less the grave effects which will accrue to the host community of the massive Newham mosque. Thus they have found it quite appropriate, and perhaps even imperative to step forward to provide this report, indeed, this in-depth study that places the mosque at the centre of the Islamic system, and describes from Islamic sources the prescribed activities condoned within a mosque. We say system rather than religion because Muslims since the days of Muhammad have emphasized that the Islamic *Shari'ah* has answers to everything in life—from politics to economics to every choice man is apt to make in his life—but more importantly, that life itself is meaningless without Islam.

The authors have taken extreme caution to produce a detailed and well-documented report from Islamic sources, whereby even Muslim scholars will be hard pressed to challenge any of its details and findings. However, there is a risk—its findings could be discounted by well-meaning Westerners and others who might not want to face the implications herein. Instead of the peaceful and tolerant model, the Islam that emerges in this study, as practiced daily in every mosque, matches that of what we hear in the news about the goals and mindsets of terrorists, suicide bombers, Al-Qaida, and the like. But aren't those people just the fringe of the Islamic society, a society noted for its tolerance, moderation, and ethical values?

Many of our well meaning leaders, whether in the UK, Washington, Paris, Berlin or Moscow, have all said very kind words about the peaceful religion of Islam, and have many political and personal relationships with Muslim leaders and businessmen whom they greatly praise and seem to admire—and these people may be indeed men of personal integrity, but they may not yet themselves be fully aware of the full implications of their own belief system. However, in time, even they will be inexorably drawn back to the core of Islamic doctrine and practice as has happened in previous centuries when Islam went on the rise again, as it has in more recent times with the 1979 Islamic revolution in Iran.

In point of fact, there is a desire in the hearts of a growing number of moderate Muslims for reform and one observes even today the growth of many Islamic reform movements, movements that would advocate a form of modernity, personal freedom, religious choice, revision of harsh Islamic laws and many others. This indeed seems welcome, but let us heed words of caution. Such movements had their rise and fall throughout Islamic history. Literally, all Islamic reform movements have ultimately been either marginalized, defeated, or eliminated. One of the great notable examples is the public burning of the Islamic philosopher Ibn-Rushd's[1] voluminous writings in Cordoba, Spain in the 13th century; even though he had held a high level position within the government as a *qadi* (judge) in the Islamic *Shari'ah* court. His writings substantiated the concept that "truth" could be found outside Islamic sources, and thus his works were considered "blasphemous," even though he was, and is still respected in many circles as a major philosopher who brought in-depth analyses of Aristotle into Europe and the Islamic world.

As terrorist attacks have subsequently proliferated worldwide these speculations in the Western press continue in an increasing crescendo questioning once more such political and military activities emanating in and through the mosque.

To put it mildly, the world today is quite confused about what they see in the name of Islam. I believe that the average Muslim is also troubled especially in the area of human rights, freedom of choice and whether Al-Qaida really represents core Islamic values. On a personal level I spent many years trying to hold on to Islam precisely because of the hope of some kind of reform. Belteshazzar and Abednego have provided a challenging work that needs to be taken seriously by Muslims and non-Muslims alike.

Perhaps, by reading between the lines in this report you may discover why Reform Islam may never make it—unlike Reform Christianity or Judaism. Believe me, I wish that I were wrong, but the facts need to be faced.

Gideon

April, 2006

---

[1] Known in the West as Averroes. He wrote extensively on the theory of knowledge and advocated a reconciliation between Islam and natural law based on Aristotle's works. The famous theologian Thomas Aquinas was his contemporary and made good use of Averroes' works to advance new ideas in the Catholic Church.

Introduction

Several articles have been appearing in the Western Press during the past decade voicing concern with the apparent role that mosques seem to be playing worldwide—beyond that of a place of worship—even prior to the infamous 9/11 Twin Towers attack in New York City, the Madrid train attack, and the more recent bus and underground train attacks in London.

For instance, both *The Times* and *The Guardian* recently wrote on the Finsbury Park mosque[2], regarding the political and military activities of certain Muslims in their midst who were later implicated in a terrorist campaign in Yemen. These articles also questioned the related role of the Madrassas that are attached to these particular mosques in the training of those individuals, and by implication, the role of madrassas in general as a possible motivation for such thought and actions.

Similar concerns are being voiced in the press and in the streets of the affected community in East London, regarding recently announced plans to build a mega-mosque there in time for the 2012 Summer Olympics.

Very few mosques in the world would match the capacity and expected architectural grandeur of the proposed Newham mosque. Such a mammoth building in a peaceful neighbourhood has understandably aroused local concerns. But are these normal concerns (affecting traffic, noise, property values—to name a few), sufficiently important to justify preventing such a mosque from being constructed? No doubt the sponsors of this project are well ahead of the game, and have already advanced a good report on the expected local and national benefits to the local community, and most likely they have already challenged the authorities to "live up to the U.K. standard of freedom of religion, worship and personal expression."

It is therefore appropriate to question and examine exactly what the mosque is, and what are its functions, and more importantly, does it improve community relations, enhance peaceful coexistence with the host community, and promote a pluralistic religious environment?

---

[2] *The Times*, 12th January 1999; *The Guardian*, 16th January 1999

This can only be told by a determination of what the sources of the Islamic worldview prescribe and advocate, based on the *Qur'an* and the *Sunnah*—as the two primary sources for Islamic doctrine—as well as the body of law which flows from these two sources, the *Shari'ah* law.

There is a progression which is illustrated both through diagrams herein and the various writings of leading authorities of Islam, as well as their juristic decree known as fatwas, which will assist the reader in understanding how the edicts which back up political and military thought and activities within the mosques come about.

By the time the various issues of the day are filtered through the hands of the *ulama* [3] in the *Shari'ah* courts and are returned back to the mosques, the various political and military activities which necessarily flow from those edicts/determinations have been vetted and set in motion. There is very very little room, if any, for independent thinking on the part of the members or leaders of the mosques at this point in time, as these rulings are binding, and are thus well beyond question.

Yet this process which ended up back at the mosque level with final edicts (see Figure 3), actually also began here at mosque level originally—in defining the current issues to be decided by the *ulama'*, in planning, in teaching, etc. For those learned men who rise from the ranks of the local mosques to become the *ulama'*, are also leaders of the mosques, preachers, scholars and judges who issue fatwas. They recite, they expound their decrees, they rule! Their office is not subject to either question or discussion having being firmly established by Qur'anic injunctions.

In putting the various pieces of the puzzle together for our readers, we will be labouring over the barriers of terminology which will sound at first to be the familiar terminology of the Judeo-Christian worldview—but a word to the wise is that this familiarity is in appearance only. So bear with us in the use of terms and our definitions of terms you may have thought that you knew.

Hence we will labour over new terminology (such as *takiyya*), and go over old terminology (such as *jihad* and *hijra*), all to reach a better and clearer understanding that in Islam—rank and file—the mosque is

---

[3] *Ulama'* are Jurists, men of knowledge authorized to interpret the *Shari'ah* as it applies to current events and issues. See Chart, page 11.

always the centre, the beginning, and the end of all Islamic affairs societally and judicially speaking in Islamic terms.

A careful read will help to dispel ignorance and enlighten the reader about one of the most crucial yet most neglected institutions of our day.

The Islamic View of Life and Religion

The relationship between life and religion in a Muslim society is foundationally different from that in other societies. In non-Muslim societies, there is a lot more to life than just "religion." Furthermore, the freedom to choose one's religion is in principle a personal matter, respected by others, and protected by law.

Life and Religion in Islam

In Islam the very idea of a "choice" is not only an anathema but it is regarded as an anti-Islamic concept. Freedom of choice does not exist; neither is religion a private nor a personal matter.

In Islam, life and religion are deeply intertwined and inseparable. If a Muslim discards his religion for another, it is regarded as the highest treason and punishable by death in Islamic law.

The issue of 'no compulsion in religion' often quoted by Muslims when freedom of religion is discussed is a convenient phrase. It is part of Sura 2, verse 256. This and other similar verses that Muhammad stated earlier in his preaching that proclaim flexibility have all been abrogated and replaced by later revelations, according to Islamic jurisprudence and revered authoritative Qur'anic expositors.[4]

If there was no compulsion in religion and that was indeed true, why does the Saudi Penal code prescribe a death penalty to any Muslim within Saudi Arabia were he to change his religion? Why is Abdul Rahman, the Afghani convert, in prison facing a death sentence for his conversion to Christianity? Why was Mehdi Debaj assassinated by Iranian government agents for converting to Christianity? Why do the Iranian authorities persecute those who convert to Ba'ahiism?

Almost anywhere in the Islamic world, a public statement of a Muslim's conversion or discarding of Islam bears a heavy penalty, of isolation, official persecution, imprisonment, and even death.

Even if one were to make a simple statement with no intention to offend that "Muhammad the prophet of Islam was not holy" or Islam is not the "final religion"; that would be regarded as blasphemous almost

---

[4] To understand why it does get quoted so often despite its being abrogated, please see the section on *takiyya*.

everywhere in the Islamic world. In Pakistan for instance one would be charged with blasphemy under Pakistan's Penal code of 295, A, B, & C with the penalty varying from minimum 10 years to life imprisonment, or even a death sentence.

The following Qur'anic verses and others like it have abrogated that often-quoted phrase "no compulsion in religion":

Sura 9:5, 11 *When the forbidden months are past then fight and kill the unbelievers wherever you find them, and seize them, beleaguer them and lie in wait for them, in every stratagem of war, but if they repent (meaning accept Islam) and establish regular prayers, and practice regular charity... then they are your brethren in religion (Islam).*

Sura 8:38-39 *Say to the unbelievers, if they desist from unbelief their past will be forgiven them, but if they persist the punishment of those before them is already a warning to them. And fight and kill them, until there is no more tumult or dissention and that everywhere religion will be unto Allah.*

Furthermore, according to Islamic jurisprudence and *Shari'ah*, with the unanimous agreement of all scholars, "no compulsion in religion" simply means that all Arabs, Jews, Christians, non-believers, and pagans have the freedom to convert to Islam but not the other way around, i.e., it is a one-way freedom. Now it is true that Muslim leaders in the West have stated that if a Muslim converts to another religion he ought not be killed, but that may have just been for media consumption. If they are serious, they should issue a proper *fatwa*[5] endorsing what is being stated and seek the same from their institutions, such as the Organisation of Islamic Conference, The Muslim World League, The Union of Islamic Ulama', or Al Azhar University in Cairo, Egypt... to name but a few.

---

[5] Official religious edict based on the Islamic *Shari'ah* and fully backed by Qur'anic and certified *Hadith* references.

Illustrations

Please look carefully at the following two illustrations. **Figure 1** demonstrates that in the non-Islamic view, religion plays only a part of life.

Figure 1: Life versus Religion in the Non-Islamic Worldview

The first rectangle is entitled life, in which religion appears to be a tiny part of that life, indicating it to be private, no matter how ardent one may be in his/her beliefs, with the full choice of when and where to worship, in setting personal prayer times, direction of prayer, kinds of food, who to associate with, etc.

Now consider **Figure 2** and compare. The Islamic view is illustrated in the second diagram whereby the whole rectangle is a religious system and life is a tiny part of it. According to the Islamic worldview, religion is everything. All that is in life emanates from religion, from the most basic personal hygiene regulations to the most major issues in the community.

Figure 2: Life versus Religion in the Islamic Worldview

Definition of Islam

Islam cannot be defined only as a religion in the Western sense of the word, neither can it be termed as a faith only. It is a *whole encompassing system*. It is first and foremost a socio-political and socio-religious system, as well as socio-economic, socio-educational, legislative, judiciary, and military system, cloaked and garbed in religious terminology, with regulations that govern every aspect of the lives of its adherents and their relationships among themselves, and with those that are non-Muslims.

The main institution that plays a central role in the Muslim community directing their lives and almost everything related to that is the mosque.

Although the terminology regarding a place of worship and other religious terms may be the same between Muslims and non-Muslims (e.g. Christians, Jews, Hindus, etc), the concepts and the definitions are radically and dramatically different. In other words, we cannot and must not view or regard Islamic concepts, doctrines and institutions as we would those of other religions; it would be a grave error and most misleading to do so.

Two Primary Components

Islam in all of its entirety is founded on two primary components:

1. The *Qur'an*: the book which Muhammad claimed to be from Allah revealed to him through Gabriel in piecemeal over a period of 23 years.

2. *Sunnah*: the example of Muhammad, which is equally important, if not more important, than the *Qur'an* itself. It consists of all of his teachings, in words, in deeds, and whatever else he consented to. This *Sunnah*, or the example of the prophet Muhammad, is indispensable for Islam. For without the *Sunnah* no Islamic practice or belief is certain, nor can the *Qur'an* itself be understood.

Since Muhammad is the highest and the most venerated model for the Muslim community, they are ordered to imitate him and obey him by many a Qur'anic injunction:

Sura 68:4 *...you O (Muhammad) are the most exalted standard of character*

Sura 53:2-5 *...your companion is neither gone astray nor misled, nor does he say anything of his own desire, it is all an inspiration sent down to him. He was taught by one mighty in power.*

Sura 33:21 *...you have indeed in the Messenger of Allah a beautiful pattern of conduct for anyone whose hope is in Allah and the last day, and who engages much in the praise of Allah*

Sura 4:80 *He who obeys the Apostle has already obeyed Allah*

Sura 48:8-10 *...we have truly sent you (Muhammad) as a witness as a bringer of glad tidings and as a warner. In order that you (people) may believe in Allah and His Messenger, that you assist him and celebrate his praises morning and evening. Verily those who pledge their fealty (absolute loyalty) do no less than pledge their fealty to Allah*

Sura 59:7 *...what Allah has restored to His messenger, having taken it away from the people of the townships, belongs to Allah and his messenger and to kindred and orphans, the needy and the wayfarer, in order that it may not make a circuit between the wealthy among you, so take what the Apostle assigns you and abstain from that he prohibits you.*

Hence, regarding any issue in Islam, the only definitive answer in any given category is what the Jurisprudence states, based on these twofold foundations, and disseminated by the mosque (See Figure 3).

The Mosque (masjid in Arabic)

The word mosque—known as *Masjid* in Arabic—is derived from the root word *sajada* or *suju,* meaning to prostrate, which is normally viewed as worship. Worship in Islam is upholding and implementing the revealed law of Allah—the *Shari'ah.*

There is no concept of personal relationship between man and Allah in Islam. The biblical teaching that God is our Father is not found in Islam. Nor is the concept of Christ dying for mankind, thus making God accessible and knowable.

The biblical concept that human beings have been created in the image of God is an anathema and an apostasy to Muslims. Hence the Christian understanding of the Fatherly love of God is unknowable in Islam. The purpose of worship in Islam is to demonstrate the submission and total surrender of a slave to his master.

This implementation of the *Shari'ah* or the revealed will and law of Allah is not a matter of choice, either, but is a matter of enforcement on themselves and others, be it willingly or unwillingly, and where it is opposed, Jihad would be necessary.

The Mosque as the Gathering Place (jama'a in Arabic)

A commonly used term for the mosque is the Arabic word, *Jama'a,* which is derived from a root word meaning to gather or gathering. It is a place where Muslims gather since a mosque's role is that of a centre of authority for the Muslim community, which guides and instructs them in their religious as well as temporal duties and obligations and directs their relationships with their environment as per the revealed Laws of Islam.

Different Kinds of Mosques

All mosques are not equal in status. These variations occur not only in theological or doctrinal differences, i.e., Shi'a versus Sunni or between Sufi and Salafi. But even within the same school the mosques vary in their importance.

These distinctions were introduced by Muhammad himself when he stated that a prayer performed in the sacred mosque, the *Ka'aba* in Mecca, is equivalent to one hundred thousand performed elsewhere. He went on to say that a prayer performed in his mosque in Medina is equivalent to one thousand prayers elsewhere, and one performed in the Al Aqsa mosque in Jerusalem is worth five hundred performed elsewhere. The same is true of Shi'ites regarding Qum, Isfahan, Mashad, Najaf and Karabala, the latter being the highest in merit.

On this and other complicated factors the Muslims have through historical importance and special initiations built a hierarchy of mosques. So two mosques in Cairo, a few miles apart, will differ in their religious importance. A prayer said in Miser al Gadida is worth much less than if it was performed in the mosque of Amer ibn Al'aas. The mosque of Sayida Zeineb is of more importance and value than a mosque two streets away.

It is not necessary to be a particularly ancient mosque to be more important. The calculation of its importance is based on many factors, both religious, political, and the content of its preaching and teaching, as well as what and who it houses. If the *Jama'at Tablighi* were to move their national and international headquarters from Pakistan, then wherever they base themselves, be it in London, Paris or elsewhere—that mosque will have both religious as well as political significance throughout the Islamic world. This is because of the pietistic fame of that mosque's founders and its members, achieved by being a radical Islamic missionary training and sending agency, its emphasis on austere living and its ideological and theological purity of 7th Century Islam.

Jama'at Tablighi has the respect and honour that it has in the Muslim community because of its being a major force in worldwide Islamic resurgence.

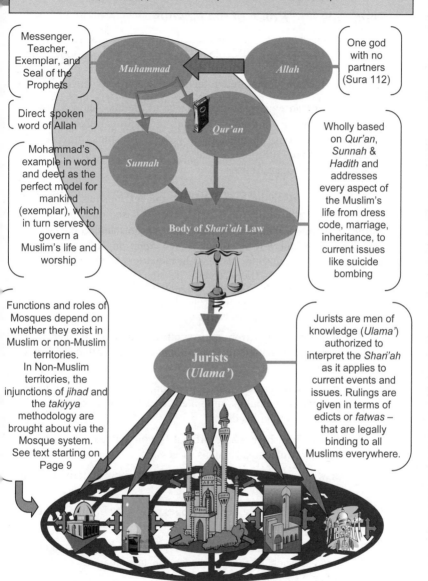

Progression of Islamic Doctrine:
Inception to Application and Implementation at the Mosque

Messenger, Teacher, Exemplar, and Seal of the Prophets

Muhammad

Allah

One god with no partners (Sura 112)

Direct spoken word of Allah

Qur'an

Wholly based on *Qur'an*, *Sunnah* & *Hadith* and addresses every aspect of the Muslim's life from dress code, marriage, inheritance, to current issues like suicide bombing

Mohammad's example in word and deed as the perfect model for mankind (exemplar), which in turn serves to govern a Muslim's life and worship

Sunnah

Body of *Shari'ah* Law

Functions and roles of Mosques depend on whether they exist in Muslim or non-Muslim territories. In Non-Muslim territories, the injunctions of *jihad* and the *takiyya* methodology are brought about via the Mosque system. See text starting on Page 9

Jurists (*Ulama'*)

Jurists are men of knowledge (*Ulama'*) authorized to interpret the *Shari'ah* as it applies to current events and issues. Rulings are given in terms of edicts or *fatwas* – that are legally binding to all Muslims everywhere.

Figure 3: The mosque as the central point for the dissemination and application of the rulings of Islamic law (the *Shari'ah*), derived from the two primary sources, the *Qur'an* and the *Sunnah*.

- 11 -

Functions and Roles of the Mosque

Every mosque attempts to be modelled on the first mosque built and directed by Muhammad in Medina. The functions of a mosque cannot be understood without considering the first mosque and its role and rule in the first Muslim community.

When Muhammad emigrated from Mecca to Medina—now known as *hijra* which has an enormous spiritual and political significance in Islam—the majority of its inhabitants were not Muslims. It had a large Jewish population, both proselytised Arabs, Jews and Christians, and a large majority of pagan Arabs.

Muhammad built a mosque on arrival in Medina even before he built his own house to demonstrate its utter importance.

As the *Shari'ah* unfolded in Medina, the mosque was to become not only a building where religious teachings were taught but also much more.

1. It was the first *madrassa* (an Islamic seminary) where Islamic doctrine was taught and whereby the companions were raised and instructed by Muhammad.

2. It was the pulpit from which spiritual admonitions were given and encouragement to resist the non-Islamic influence through *jihad*.

3. It was here that the *jihad* operations were discussed, directed and its commanders appointed, both by Muhammad and his successors after his death.

4. It was from here where official Islamic delegations were sent both by Muhammad and his successors.

5. It was where the delegations and the representatives of the tribes were received.

6. It was in this mosque the pledges of loyalty of the Arab tribes to Muhammad and Islam were received.

7. It was where the affairs of the Islamic state were conducted and, as such at the time, was the headquarters of the first Islamic state as well as a mosque.

8. It was here that *jihad* was proclaimed and from here the Muslim armies were sent to conquer the world.

9. It was in this mosque that Mohammad's companions were recognised and honoured for their achievements and were encouraged to pursue the enemies of Islam and eliminate all opposition.

10. It was here that Muhammad and his successors, Abu Bakr, Omar, Uthman and Ali appointed judges for the different regions and the commanders of military troops, and where Jihad detachments were dispatched and high-ranking state officials and tax collectors were sent.

11. It was here that the contracts, pacts and treaties were commissioned.

12. It was here where the Islamic *Shari'ah* unfolded, where the binding, and loosing, permitting and prohibiting was declared.

13. It was here the superiority of the Muslims and the inferiority of non-Muslims was declared.

14. It was here the supremacy of man over a woman and the inequality among people was taught.

15. Saddest of all, it was here where death sentences were issued to those who had opposed Muhammad or had spoken of him unfavourably, and from here the ardent soldiers set off to implement these death sentences.

16. It was in that mosque those culprits who eliminated Muhammad's enemies were highly praised and honoured by their prophet. Examples include:

    a. Omeyer bin Al Khatem, who brutally killed A'sma bint Marwan as she was breast-feeding her baby

    b. Abdallah bin Anis, for assassinating Sufyan bin Khalid

    c. Saleem Bin Amaeyer, for killing Abu Affaq the Jew

    d. Abdallah bin Attiq, for killing a Jew called Ibn Abi Haqqiq

    e. Ali bin Abi Talib, for killing A'Nader ibn Harith.

17. Finally it was from this mosque that Muslim armies marched out to conquer and thus change the face of the world.

The Contemporary Mosque and its Role

All Muslims are under obligation and required to emulate Muhammad in word and deeds. For this is a divine decree and an indispensable doctrinal pillar of Islam.

Muhammad spent 13 years of a total of 23 years of his mission in Mecca. During these 13 years, he never ever built a mosque or described any of its functions.

Although prayer is mentioned in the Meccan section of the *Qur'an*, there was no Islamic form of prayer in Mecca as we know it today. This came in Medina.

Naturally, then, a question arises: how and where did the early Muslim community pray during the first 13 years of early Islam?

Muslims know very little, if anything, regarding the status of a mosque during the Islamic formative period in Mecca, for this remains shrouded in secrecy.

Muslim scholars have attempted to explain away the absence of a mosque in Mecca during the early Islamic period by saying that the *Ka'aba* was the mosque but, as it was under the control of the pagan Arabs, Muhammad and his companions could not pray there until it was purged and purified from all the idols in and around it. This required political powers which he did not have then, neither had he the military force that it required to subdue the pagans. So in their view, it had to come in stages, the revelations in Medina, building of the first mosque, obtaining political power through military strength, then conquering Mecca.

It is clear that the very first mosque in Medina was first and foremost a political office: its combined function was a socio-religious as well as a socio-political outlet.

Based on this and the pattern set by Muhammad of his very first mosque, a modern mosque must model itself on that of Medina.

Examples from Recent History

Hence, besides the normal socio-religious and socio-educational functions of a mosque, we would be considering a mosque in its political role. Here are some examples from different periods of recent history and from different locations of what Islamic scholars have said regarding a mosque's political role.

Cairo: In that very fashion, as Muhammad sent forth his armies for Jihad from the mosque in Medina, so the scholars of Al Azhar mosque, Abdallah al Sharqawi and Ahmed Aldardair led the Egyptians against the French occupation. The Al Azhar also had a major role in the 1919 Revolt against the British, so much so that the British forces were stationed outside Al Azhar mosque to prevent any of its scholars or students from taking further part in the demonstrations.

So later did Hassan Al Banna and his men engage in *jihad* and, later still, the Gamma Islamiya to such an extent that the Egyptian government was forced to close down many mosques.

Transjordan: In 1936, the Kasim Revolution was inaugurated in Al Istiklal mosque in Palestine. It was in this mosque that all their secret organization and all its various committees were housed.

West Bank and Gaza: It was the mosque that played the most major role in whipping up the first and the second Intifada. The Khatibees, the sermon preachers of the Al Aqsa mosque in Jerusalem, had a central role in inciting *jihad* against Jews and the state of Israel.

An independent news report of 30th November 2003 points out that most of the mosques in the West Bank and Gaza are centres and instigators of violence against Israel rallied on through the Friday sermons and distributing hate leaflets and materials published by Hamas and Islamic Jihad. The report particularly focuses on Al E'in mosque in Ramallah as a model and leader in organization and recruitment of suicidal mission candidates. One of the activists—a wanted terrorist—was even sheltered in Abdel Nasser mosque in Ramallah. The mosque continues to play a major role in the present Intifada.

Finsbury Park Mosque and Others

The events and activities that took place both at the Finsbury Park mosque and the New Jersey mosque are not new. Outwardly it may look as an indictment of the personal activities of Abu Hamza and that of Sheikh Omar Abel Rahman. But the more one examines this the more one comes across that same recurrence in so many other places. So it is in Iraq today where the mosques are at the heart of inciting violence and the killing of the enemies of Islam, particularly Americans and Europeans. What is seen and termed as Islamic resurgence would have not been possible without the involvement of the mosque.

It is no different in Egypt, Pakistan, India, Indonesia, Nigeria, Sudan, Algeria, Bangladesh and elsewhere. Wherever one looks, the mosque continues to play its role as prescribed by the first mosque. The examples given from different periods and countries demonstrates the consistency of the argument.

Political Role of the Mosque According to the Shari'ah

Regarding the mosque and it political role, a *fatwa* issued by Sheikh Yousif Al Qardawi on the 29th October 2001 states:

...in the life of the prophet there was no distinction between what the people call sacred and secular or religion and politics, and he had no place other than the mosque for politics and other related issues. So that he would establish this precedent for his religion and for the world.

The mosque at the time of the prophet was his propagation centre, the headquarters of the State, as it was for his successors, the rightly guided Khalifas, the mosque was their base for all their activities political as well as non-political. Politics as a science is one of the best disciplines, and as a practice and career it's the most honourable. The surprising thing is that it's the politicians, who are totally immersed in it from the top of their heads to the sole of their feet, that are enquiring if the mosque should embark and leap into political affairs. Politics in itself is neither vice, nor evil in itself, according Islam. As Muslims it is part of our religion, for it is doctrine and worship. A system for the whole of life... and the mission of the mosque as required by correct Islam is not an isolation from the politics in this sense, but the mosque is to command the Muslims on all that would produce good in their religion and world and through the mosque the people learn the truth and goodness. The mosque must then have a role in guiding the nation and informing her about the critical issues and making her see her enemies. From ancient times the mosque has had a role in jihad for the sake of Allah, resisting the enemies of this religion from the invading occupiers. That blessed Intifada in the land of the prophets, Palestine, started from none other but the mosques and its first call came from the minarets and it was first known as the mosque revolution. The mosque's role in the Afghan jihad, and every Islamic jihad (its role) cannot be denied.[6]

Qardawi's *fatwa* is rooted in the Islamic *Shari'ah* and it is a clear directive and explicit incitement to the call to violence under the banner of resistance. What Qardawi is stating is that the mosque has been and will continue to be the same, and that the minarets will continue to call for *jihad*. But why?

The Entire Earth Is a Mosque

Muhammad said that the earth had been declared to him a mosque and pure (ceremonial purity); in another report, it has been stated that the earth had been declared to him purged, purified and a mosque. This saying of Muhammad's is reported by Bukhari and Muslim, both renowned *Hadith* scholars and revered authorities.[7]

In practical terms, this means Muhammad and his followers are to conquer the whole world and cleanse it, purge it from all kinds of *kufr*, meaning apostasy. Therefore, the mosque's mission or function is not to be limited to prayer and religious services only, but extends to physically and practically how to bring the earth under Islamic dominion.

Muslims believe that Islam is a universal religion with a universal mission, a message to be proclaimed to all mankind.

Sura 7:158 *Say (O Muhammad): O mankind! Lo! I am the messenger of Allah to you all...*

Sura 34:28 *And We have not sent thee (O Muhammad) save as a bringer of good tidings and a warner unto all mankind; but most of mankind know not.*

Sura 3:20 *Say unto the people of the book have you surrendered? If they were to be Muslims then they are guided...*

---

[6] This fatwa is online at the following address:
http://www.qaradawi.net/site/topics/article.asp?cu_no=2&item_no=3598&version=1&template_id=230&parent_id=17
http://www.islamonline.net/servlet/Satellite?cid=1122528600828&pagename=IslamOnline-Arabic-Ask_Scholar/FatwaA/FatwaAAskTheScholar

[7] This is Hadith #31901, Kanz al Umal.

Islam believes in its own universality and as "The Only Religion of Allah", and that Muslims are commanded to bring the whole world under subjugation to Islam.

Under the laws of subjugation in Islam, non-Muslims are given a choice either to convert to Islam or pay a hefty tax, which is paid publicly. While paying this tax, the payee would be humiliated for remaining an unbeliever. Politically, he/she would not have equal rights, neither would the non-Muslims be regarded as equal citizens and treated as such in all fields of employment, housing, and positions of authority. This, of course, is the norm and has been for nearly fourteen centuries in all Islamic countries where the Christians are a minority.

This subjugation is first and foremost a recognition of Islam's political hegemony over all other systems and as such its superiority must be accepted.

Then, as a superior system both religiously and politically, mosques are erected everywhere. In Islamic countries, other faiths are prohibited from proclaiming as well as building their worship outlets: the building of churches and like are strictly controlled and limited.

In this way, the mosque remains a mark and symbol of the religious and political identity of the people.

Sura 3:19 *...the religion before Allah is Islam*

Sura 3:83 *Do they seek for other than the religion of Allah? While all creatures have, willingly or unwillingly, accepted Islam*

Sura 3:85 *If anyone desires a religion other than Islam, Never will it be accepted of him in this life and in the hereafter he will be in the ranks of those who have lost and condemned*

Figure 4 (overleaf) explains it best, where the whole world is in the mosque. The question then, is, can there be any other religious building in the mosque?

To purge the earth and bring it under subjugation, Muhammad ordered his men to engage in Jihad. This is because Islam views the world as either Islamic or non-Islamic.

The Islamic term given is *Dar Al Islam*, that is the House or Abode of Islam.

The non-Islamic world is known as *Dar Al Harb*, the House or Abode of War. But as the whole world has been given to Muhammad as a mosque, it needs to be purged and the word of Islam and its authority must be supreme.

Figure 4: Illustration whereby the entire world is a mosque

Building Blocks for the Spread of Islam

Islam has provided the means and legal systems to manage non-Muslims in Islamic lands, to give them a form of security without threatening the Muslim community through a separate but unequal status; *Dar Al-Islam*, the House of Islam, lands where Muslims are in political control.

But the task is different in lands where non-Muslims are in political control (*Dar Al-Harb*, the House of War). Although the ultimate goal is to transform the *Dar Al Harb* into *Dar Al Islam*, there are a host of intermediate goals to establish the Muslim community in the host country and help it grow. A typical intermediate goal would be to legalize some forms of the *Shari'ah* law (starting with the dress code, and continuing through *Shari'ah* family law on marriage/inheritance, etc.). In this section we describe the building blocks of how Islam can be spread and consolidated in such lands, whereby the mosque system is central in the overall process. The building blocks consist of (a) Call for *jihad*, (b) Migration into the non-Muslim lands and (c) application of the *takiyya* doctrine to avoid exposing the hidden intents of Muslim communities. We say "building blocks" because the order of use of such blocks depends on the conditions on the ground. Muhammad used a deliberate combination of slow and fast tracks depending on the relative strengths of the Muslim community.

Jihad as the Driving Principle

Abu Ala Maududi, one of the modern, most leading Islamic scholars in the Indian sub-continent, stated in his speech delivered on Iqbal Day, 13th April 1939, and later repeated in his book *Jihad in the cause of Allah*:[8]

If Islam were to be a palm tree like any other and the Muslims as a nation like any other nations of the world, then there is no crime if the Islamic jihad were to lose all its privileges and speciality that made jihad the pinnacle of all worship and the jewel of her crown. However, the truth is that Islam isn't just like any other palm tree, neither are the Muslims a nation like any other nations of the world.

---

[8] Now published by the Holy Koran Publishing House; Beirut, Lebanon.

In reality Islam is a revolutionary ideology, a revolutionary programme (agenda) to alter the social order of the whole world, and rebuild it in conformity with its own tenets and the ideals.

'Muslim' is a title of that International revolutionary party organised by Islam to carry into effect its revolutionary programme. And jihad refers to that revolutionary struggle and utmost exertion which the Islamic party brings into play to achieve this objective.

Islam wished to destroy all States and Governments anywhere on the face of the earth which are opposed to the ideology and programme of Islam, regardless of the country or the Nation which rules it. The purpose of Islam is to set up a State on the basis of its own ideology and programme regardless of which nation assumes the role of the standard bearer of Islam or the rule of which nation undermined in the process of the establishment of an ideological Islamic state.

No one has the right to become self-appointed ruler of men and issue orders and prohibitions on his own volition and authority. To acknowledge the personal authority of a human being as the source of commands and prohibitions is tantamount to admitting him as the sharer in the powers and authority of God. And this is the root of all evilness in the universe.

Islam is not merely a religious creed or compound name for a few forms of worship, but a comprehensive system which envisages to annihilate all tyrannical and evil systems in the world and enforces its own programme of reform which it deems best for the well being of mankind.

It must be evident to you from this description that the objective of Islamic jihad is to eliminate the rule of an Un-Islamic system and establish in it stead an Islamic system of State rule. Islam does not intend to confine this revolution to a single state or a few countries: the aim of Islam is to bring about a universal revolution.

Islamic jihad does not seek to interfere with the faith ideology, rituals of worship or social customs of the people.

However, Islamic jihad does not recognize their right to administer State affairs according to a system which in the view of Islam is evil. Furthermore, Islamic jihad also refuses to their right to continue with such practices under an Islamic government which fatally affect the public interest from the viewpoint of Islam.

In Islam, *jihad* takes many forms: its definition cannot be confined only to waging war with arms. Even the armed struggle needs other kinds of support. Here is a list of the various forms of *jihad* as recorded in the *Shari'ah*:

Jihad bi al lisan: *jihad* by tongue/preaching/proclaiming/debating/dialoguing.

A' jihad bi al kalam: *jihad* by pen, writing/publishing/ mass media.

A' jihad bil hijra: *jihad* by immigration, both abroad and from city to city.

A' jihad bi al mal: *jihad* through financial activities.

A' jihad bi al nafs: *jihad* in one's being.

A' jihad a' nafas: *jihad* through one's being, self-sacrifice, as in suicidal missions.

These are further sub-divided into sub-categories. We will now turn our attention to what is of immediate relevance to us in the West.

Hijra *(Migration from Mecca to Medina by Muhammad and his followers)*

We will only concern ourselves here with a social *jihad*: that of *hijra*, or migration.

This notion is important and has both religious and political significance attached to it because the *hijra*, the immigration of Muhammad from Mecca to Medina.

Migration is legally obligatory on a Muslim as preparatory to other forms of *jihad* for the victory of Islam and Muslims in other countries. This was established when Muhammad said:

I command you with these five which Allah has charged me with: assemble, listen, obey, hijra and jihad.[9]

---

[9] Tafseer al Qur'an, ibn Kathir; Dar al A'hiya a'turath al Arabi, Volume 1, p. 103. Masnad al Ansar, Imam Ahmed; Dar al A'hiya a'turath al Arabi, Volume 6, p. 471. Sunnan a' Tirmizi, Dar al Kittab, 1994. Volume 8, p. 135.

Thus he declared *hijra* as preparatory as well as pairing it with *jihad*. Muhammad further added migration to continue as long as the enemy is fighting, in other words resisting Islam. *Hijra*, migration, is obligatory as long as *kufr* or apostasy abounds.

Sura 8:72 *...those who believed and adopted immigration and fought for Islam with their wealth and their persons in the cause of Allah*

Sura 8:75 *...and those who accept faith subsequently and adopt exile and fight for the religion of Islam in your company they are of you...*

Sura 2:218 *...those who believed and those who suffered immigration and fought, strove and struggled in the cause of Allah, they have the hope of the Mercy of Allah*

Sura 9:20 *...those who believed and suffered migration, and strive with might and main in Allah's cause, with their wealth and their persons, have the highest rank in the sight of Allah: they are the people who will be winners.*

So migration precedes *jihad* and both are inextricably linked.

Collective migration, or the congregating in one area, brings in the awareness of an Islamic identity: it enables Islam to be noticed in the abode of apostasy, through its demands and refusal to integrate, and assimilate, and it helps to change and dismantle and finally annihilate the existing socio-political system of that society, as described by Madudi.[10]

In other words, it is not possible to consolidate the Islamic religion without migration. There is no way to raise the profile of Islam in the abode of apostasy without the help of Muslims and the increase of their numbers.

This increase of numbers does not have to be from one country to another; it could, if necessary, be within the same country. So migration can be from Liverpool to London, or from Leeds to Luton, if the numbers would strengthen a given area and the *kufr* there would be defeated, or at least if Islam would gain both religiously and politically.

So the grand mosque at Newham may not be needed, but such edifices are to prove a point more than its actual usage or need.

---

[10] Ibid.

This is validated by various declarations, fatwas, and statements by many Muslim scholars.

As Sheikh Qardawi declared in his *fatwa* issued on the 27th of February 2005:

> *Despite the pessimism within the ranks of Muslims, at the end, Islam will rule and will be the lord of the whole world. One of the signs of victory will be that Rome will be conquered, Europe will be occupied, Christians will be defeated and Muslims will increase and as such will be a force that will control the whole European continent.*[11]

This is what Najmadin Erbakan, the so-called moderate Turkish ex-Prime Minister, said when he addressed a German journalist:

> *You think we Muslim Turks come here only for employment and to gather the crumbs of your money. No, we are coming here to take control of your country and by being rooted here, and then building what we see as appropriate, and all that, with your consent and according to your laws.*[12]

Most of the Islamic publications in England make precisely the same point.

For instance, *Islamic Movement in the West* by Khurram Murad addresses this issue in the question "What is an Islamic movement?" He defines it as:

> *...an organized struggle to change the existing society into an Islamic society based on the Qur'an and the Sunna and make Islam, which is a code for entire life, supreme and dominant, especially in the socio-political spheres.*

Murad goes on to say:

> *...but it would be equally tragic if the tall and noble claims to the objective of a world-wide revolution and the ushering in of a new era are reduced to mere fulfilment of religious and educational needs. After all, these needs have always been catered for, in varying degrees, by various people. There was no*

---

11 http://www.islamonline.net/Fatwa/arabic/FatwDisplay.asp?hFatwaID=2042

12 http://www.elaph.com/ElaphWriter/2004/11/23948.htm

need to launch an Islamic movement for merely meeting community needs.

...despite its seeming unattainability, the movement in the West should reaffirm and re-emphasise the concept of total change and supremacy of Islam in the Western society as its ultimate objective and allocate to it the highest priority.

As mosques are the centre of the community and almost all its functions, what is being suggested can only be implemented through their leadership, and when sanctioned by them.

Qur'anic Injunctions for a Viable Survival (takiyya)

Despite the overtly cruel, harsh and intolerant Qur'anic views towards the 'others', namely Jews and Christians, there are injunctions in the Qur'an that enable the Islamic community to disguise, play down, and ,when necessary, deny both the intensity and the validity of these anti-Semitic and anti-Christian teachings of its religious system.

This particular injunction is *takiyya*, which permeates almost all the activities and dealings of Muslims within non-Muslim societies, be they religiously sacred or religiously temporal, secular or civic, since as we have seen, Islam does not distinguish between sacred and secular.

Takiyya

Takiyya means "caution, fear, or disguise." It permits the suspension, as the need arises, of almost any or all religious requirements—including a total denial of faith—when fearing threat, injury or compulsion of any kind in a non-Muslim society, or even in a Muslim society.

The Qur'anic injunction for *takiyya* is:

Sura 16:106 *Anyone who after accepting faith in Allah utters unbelief/kuffur except under compulsion, his heart remaining firm in faith but such as open their breast to unbelief, on them is wrath from Allah.*

This verse was given to Muhammad when one of his followers in Mecca, Ammar bin Yasir, was made to worship the Qurayshi idols and listen to the denigration of Muhammad, yet his heart was at ease. So according to Qur'anic expositors, this verse was revealed to put Yasir's conscience at ease and rest, with its application to every Muslim. See also:

Sura 3:28 *...let not the believers take for friends unbelievers rather than believers. If any do that, in nothing will there be help from Allah; except by way of precaution that ye may guard yourselves from them But Allah cautions you Himself...*

The word 'guard' in the phrase 'guard yourselves from them' is known as *takiyya*.

In addition to allowing the denial of faith in case of need, the Qur'anic injunctions make it both a permitted alleviation as well as an obligation as per Sura 3:28, sited above.

This obligation legitimises all activities in words and deeds contrary to what one might hold within: for example, to display love outwardly but inwardly to hate, or to evince loyalty outwardly but inwardly to feel enmity—all for the cause of Allah.

So, for instance, Al Zamakhshari, one of the most notable Islamic scholars and Qur'anic expositors, explains that how one could outwardly display loyalty and friendship while the heart inwardly would remain full of hate and enmity until either the obstructing factors are removed or the Islamic community is so secularly strong to launch an open attack.

Fakharadin A'razi states that if a Muslim fears those unbelievers amongst whom he may be because of their excessive power and strength, then he needs to pledge loyalty and love outwardly on condition that he inwardly would object to what he himself is saying; in other words, he would be saying the opposite to all that he inwardly believed.

As an addition to *takiyya*, Muhammad sanctioned lying by saying that Allah will not hold a Muslim accountable when he lies in these three situations:

- when in war, espionage, concealment, or in weakness
- with his wife, or a wife with her husband
- when reconciling or maintaining peace

Muhammad went on to say, "War is deception."

This deception can be practised at a personal level as well as at community level through its leaders and institutions.

Takiyya is practised by all Muslims, Sunni and Shi'ites alike, and all other Islamic sects, but because it's more vocalised by the Shi'ites in their teachings than the others, some think that it is exclusively a Shi'ite doctrine.

It has been reported that, Ali, the fourth Khalifa said "it is a mark of belief to prefer justice if it injures you, and injustice if it is of use to you."

Takiyya can be practiced if it is necessary, even when under oath.

Sura 2:225 *Allah will not call you to account for thoughtlessness in your oaths, but for the intention in your hearts...*

Sura 5:89 *Allah will not call you to account for what is futile in your oaths but He will call you to account for your deliberate oaths. For expiation, feed ten indigent persons, on the scale of the average for the fools of your families, or clothe them, or give a slave his freedom. If that is beyond your means fast for three days: that is the expiation for the oaths you have sworn, but keep to your oaths...*

The wiles used in connection with *takiyya*, especially in oaths with a complete mental blockage by the user, continues to do incalculable damage and injury to all of its victims.

For instance, in Pakistan, numerous Muslims, backed by mosques, have under oath accused innocent Christians, Hindus and others of blaspheming Muhammad. Others, having burned or torn pages of the Qur'an, then presented it as evidence of blasphemy, as though committed by those non-Muslims, namely Christians, either for personal gain or *jihad* against that community. Many of these victims have spent years in horrible conditions behind bars, while families became outcasts, losing their jobs and livelihoods. Almost all had to go in hiding and move from where they originally lived.

In the recent crisis of the Danish cartoons some Muslims themselves added more cartoons to those that they were rioting about, which showed Muhammad in a worse light. They then showed these to fellow Muslims in order to whip up frenzy and violence against Europeans. Many were killed in a number of Islamic countries, and many others lost their livelihood as their businesses were burnt down by Muslims.

How can a Muslim do that? There is a *fatwa*—an Islamic juristic decree—endorsing the insult of Muhammad if done in the state of *takiyya*.[13]

Takiyya permits Muslims to bow before an idol in a state of *takiyya*[14], and the desertion of regular and legislated prayers is permitted if under *takiyya*.[15]

To understand how *Takiyya* affects mosques, we need to look at what the Islamic jurists have said and the kinds of *fatwa* that are issued in that connection.

---

[13] This was issued in India and it can be found in *Fatwas of Kadikhan al fur ghani al hanafi* 489, the Indian fatwas published in Beirut by Dar al A'hiya a'turath al Arabi.

[14] The compilation of the Qur'anic injunctions by Kartabi, Section 10:180.

[15] Kartabi 10:180 ff.

The Role of Mosques in the West

Outwardly it may seem that the role of a mosque in the West might be as in the Islamic world. However, this is only true to a very limited degree.

The role that mosques play in the West is much more critical than in the Arab and Islamic world.

In the Islamic world a mosque is in the House of Islam where, generally Islam is regarded as the religion of the State and the *Shari'ah* is the main source of all legislation and almost all political posts that matter can only be held by Muslims.

Here the others, the non-Muslims, are regarded as *dhimmis,* unequal with Muslims, and have fewer rights than Muslims. However, while in the West, they are in the House of War, and thus on a war footing as their religion does not rule overall but is regarded more of a personal and private matter.

Muslim scholars have tried to soften the impact of this doctrine by stating that if Muslim are given their rights and not persecuted it would be called *Dar a' Sulh*—the House of Reconciliation. However, due to the clash of ideology, Islam being a totalitarian system within a free society, the Western system is increasingly viewed as anti-Islamic and thus a House of War.

Being on war footing requires the suspension of all normal Islamic rules and regulations. It also legitimizes special jurisprudence promulgated for such circumstances.

Inwardly the mosque and the Muslim communities suffer from their own internal divisions: identity problems, socio-political freedoms viewed from an Islamic point of view, fragmentation as a result of internal divisions, and finally the responsibility of raising sound Muslims in a non-Muslim environment, as well as consolidating the new converts from the host society. Nevertheless, let's consider the issues that exist.

1. Identity

In the Islamic states Muslims are in majority and thus, socially speaking, have no identity crisis, while in the West, Muslims face quite an upheaval, especially dealing with socio-religious issues asserting the rights of Muslims in the school curriculum, dress code, and fearing the socio-religious impact of the host society on their children and their societies.

The West, with its concept of egalitarianism, is also a problem within Western society, particularly concerning equality of all peoples before the Law, since Islam does not regard all people as equal; nor does it grant equality before the *Shari'ah* courts between a Muslim male and a Muslim female or between a Muslim and a non-Muslim.

Above all it doesn't hold the concept of freedom of religion, but holds and believes in the utmost superiority of Islam above all others both religiously and politically, which has serious legal implications on a day-to-day basis. Since freedom of religion is a core commitment in free societies, Islam is left with a serious identity crisis on all those fronts.

2. Socio-Political Freedoms

Conflicts arise over personal and family laws: forced marriages, polygamy, female circumcision, alimony, divorce, child custody, mixed marriages where the state does not grant a Muslim father an automatic custody of the children and where the right of the wife to alimony is not according to the *Shari'ah*, which is very biased toward men.

3. Fragmentation

Fragmentation exits along ethnic lines as well as between religious denominations. Religious denominational fragmentation is due to having Muslims from all sorts of Islamic schools of thoughts, and factions—Sunnis, Shi'a, Ahmadiyas, Qadiyanis, Wahabis, Salafis, Qur'anioon, Sufis as well as further divisions. Take for instance the Shi'a; within them would be Fivers, Seveners, Twelvers, Ismaelis, Khojas, Buharas, etc, etc.

Within the Sufis there are many *tarikas* or orders, branches, methods, ways.

Ethnic fragmentation is similar to this with the host community and the environment generally. Here the problem is of consolidation of their own, as well as both winning converts and influencing decision makers to be more disposed towards the Islamic agenda. Making Islam palatable to the host community is another serious challenge to Muslims.

4. Total Dominance

Finally, there is the ongoing struggle of how to achieve total dominance of the host society—as portrayed by *The Islamic Movement in the West* by the late Khuram Murad.

Regulations governing the Admission of Unbelievers in Mosques

Fatwa #26104, issued on 28th Ramadan 1423 A.H., 15th March 2002:

Petition: In New Zealand, religion and ethnic studies are a part of school curriculum. As a result, every year schools write applying to visit various churches, Buddhist temples and mosques. Is it permissible for us to allow them to enter our mosques, noting that both boys and girls come together, and some say, that some of those girls may be in their menstrual cycle, though we briefly try to explain to them about Islam, ceremonial purity, prayer and Oneness of Allah?

Fatwa: We praise Allah and prayers and blessings be on the Apostle of Allah and his companions, and hereafter; the scholars differed among themselves as listed below in four categories as to the matter of the unbelievers gaining access or entering mosques with the exception of their entrance to the holy mosque of Mecca, where they are in full agreement that none of them should ever be allowed to enter that holy mosque.

1) They must be absolutely banned from entering any part of a mosque, as stated by Kartabi and with that Omar bin Abdel Aziz wrote to his workers as reported by Ahmed Mardawi, said substantiating it: Sura 24:36 and the entrance of the kafirs is in contradiction of lifting Allah's praise.

2) The Shafi'iee school's position is that they are to be allowed to enter all mosques with the exception of holy mosques in Arabia.

3) The Maliki school's position is that they are to be forbidden from entering any mosque except for necessity.

4) They may be allowed to enter mosques if permitted by the Muslims there.

5) It's permissible for the unbeliever to be given permission to enter mosques if that is useful and beneficial and in the favour of the Muslim community.[16]

Pope's visit to the Umayyad Mosque

Fatwa #8250, issued on 28th Safar 1422 A.H., 25th March 2001:

Petition: Is it permissible for the Pope to pray in the Umayyad mosque or even to enter it?

Fatwa: Praise be to Allah and prayers and peace be upon the Apostle of Allah and his companions and hereafter: the rules governing a kaffir and his entrance of a mosque has been given in Fatwa 4041 in which we explained the difference of opinion among the ulama'. With the conclusion that it is possible for the kaffir to enter any mosque, with exception of the holy mosque, if that was necessary or if in their entrance there was a benefit for Islam such as the kaffir's conversion. But that does not mean that the head of crusading apostasy to be allowed to defile the mosques of the Muslims, for he is the one leading the christening and misleading astray the poor and needy Muslims to apostasy, manipulating their need for feed, drink and medicine.

How could he be allowed to enter the mosques of Muslims when he is the head of the Christianity that fights the Muslims all over the World. There is no need and no benefit in his entry of the mosque.

And hosting him is not to invite him to Islam, and there is no need to pursue that either.

For the entry of an apostate in the mosque is to hear Islam. Or to do repair work or maintenance is one colour...

But coming into the mosque with the pretence of tolerance and that he bears a message of understanding between those who say that Allah is a three of the third and those who believe in Oneness is another colour.

Some of them claim that the followers of the three religions all have the same common ground, i.e. belief in God, and the last day,

---

[16] http://webcache.dmz.islamweb.net.qa/ver2/Fatwa/ShowFatwa.php?lang=A&Id=26104&Option=FatwaId

prophecy, and the book and they all can stand together in the face of atheism and the non-religious, ignoring what the apostasy that the Christians and the Jews are in ….and it has been decided that it is not permissible for a kaffir to assert and practice the symbolism of his apostasy in the houses of Allah which are established to proclaim His oneness. [17]

Non-Muslim Sponsorships of Mosques

Fatwa #6261, issued on 16th Safar 1420, 17th April 1999:

Petition: What is the view of the *Shari'ah* that an atheistic foreign body wants to sponsor and participate building a mosque for the Muslims in France? Noting that the Muslims are well able to achieve that without any foreign intervention.

Fatwa: Praise be to Allah and prayers and peace be upon the Apostle of Allah and his companions, here after, the patronage of kaffirs in their partnership with the Muslims to build a mosque is limited to one of these three possibilities.

1) Their partnership in responsibility such that they the kaffirs would have a say in the affairs of the mosque and its administration. This is not permissible and it is forbidden because in it is their partnership in the religion of the Muslims and their worship while remaining in their state of unbelief, kufur would be lording over the Muslims.

2) It could be a technical partnership in the planning of the building and the likes of it, is not allowed unless that expertise is found among that Muslim community because the kaffirs are enemies of this religion and its followers. Thus, they can not be trusted for it; if they were to oversee it being built, they hide what would be damaging or offensive to Muslims, but if they participated because there was no other option or because previously it was one of their churches or it was a public building and the Muslims bought it, then the prayers of the Muslims in it are acceptable.

3) Financial partnership in the form that they would offer finances to the Muslims to build mosque without any strings attached, then there is no objection. For the prophet accepted presents from the kaffirs

---

[17] http://www.islamweb.net.ver2/Fatwa/ShowFatwa.php?lang=A&Id=8250 &Option=FatwaID

such as Qasir the Roman Emperor, the Makus and as such, it is permissible for a Muslim to accept such presents from the kaffirs and use it or place it in the mosque, if appropriate, and would be beneficial to the Muslims.[18]

Non Islamic Prayer in a Mosque

Fatwa #7262, issued 26th Zu le Hejja 1421 A.H, 5th April 2000:

Petition: Is it permissible to hold a mass or Christian prayer in an Islamic mosque?

Fatwa: Praise be to Allah and prayers and peace be upon the Apostle of Allah and his companions, and here after. Not either Christians nor any other kaffirs are allowed to hold any of their prayers or religious services inside a mosque. These are some of the most serious vices over which no one should be quiet.

For how can that be allowed in the houses of Allah in which Allah's remembrance is commanded and that must be only to Him.

Sura 71:18 …and in the end He will return you into the earth and raise you forth

Sura 24:36 …in Houses which Allah hath permitted to be raised to honour, for the celebration in them of His name in them is he glorified.

Sura 2:125 Remember, we made the house a place of assembly for men and a place of safety, and take ye the station of Abraham as a place of prayer. And we covenanted with Abraham and Ismael that they should sanctify my house for those who compass it round, or use it as a retreat, or bow or prostrate themselves there in prayer.

And the prophet ordered the cleansing of the Ka'aba from all the idols in it and around it, and forbad the pagans from cicumcirling it and he ordered to be proclaimed no pagan from this year onwards to perform pilgrimage and no naked person will circumlate the house meaning Ka'aba.[19]

---

[18] http://www.islamweb.net/ver2/Fatwa/ShowFatwa.php?lang=A&Id=6261 &Option+FatwaId

[19] http://www.islamweb.net/ver2Fatwa/ShowFatwa.php?lang=A&Id=7262 &Option+fatwId

Non-Muslim Officiating a Mosque Opening

Fatwa #26159, issued 17th Ramadan 1421A.H., 5th April 2000:

Petition: We built a mosque from donations, most of which has come from the local authority, and now we have invited the Mayor to officiate its opening. Is this permissible by the *Shari'ah*?

Fatwa: Praise be to Allah and prayers and peace be upon the Apostle of Allah and his companions, then after. The whole life of the prophet was and is a lesson, we depend on it as source of light and revelation, added to the daily immolation, we draw from it principles and guidance for he is the highest and most honoured in every sense of the word. Here we draw a lesson from the Hudaybiya incident. Hudiybia jurisprudence is all about concessions and balancing. How and when can it be? It is the appropriateness of making the right political decisions that would render benefits to Islam and Muslims.

The Hudibya jurisprudence is the best example of understanding of loyalty and disavowal where one party fully wants to do the will of Allah and be obedient to Him as per his revealed Shari'ah, while the other is full of Kuffur and in enmity with Allah. The apostle of Allah's success in planning cunningly and dependence on Allah to out-manoeuvre his enemies on their terms.

1) When he undertook the Hudibyia mission, he called all the Arabs and their armies to march with him to Mecca. Those that were held back by the affairs of this world thought that he would not go until they were ready but he left with those that were ready to go with him, Ansar, Muhajerun and whoever else joined him.

The Apostle of Allah made concessions to obtain renunciation from them of their own rights, using not only Muslims but pagans, too, responding positively to the demands of the kaffirs.

Thus, not all concessions to the enemy are to be rejected. Neither accepting the terms or demands of the enemy is vice. The wisdom in that is to gain the maximum with giving away the most minimum, yet achieving the victory of Islam overcoming the corruption of the Kufer. The pagans put the most intolerable barriers by forbidding the Muslims to preamble the agreement with "Bismillah al rahamin a' rahim", "In the name Allah, the most gracious, the most merciful". Though the Muslims refused it, the Apostle, in his wisdom surmounted it by his acceptance of it. They even refused his basic but most honourable title Muhammad, The Apostle of Allah: instead, he wrote 'Muhammad bin Abdul Allah'.

Hardness and harshness, violence and hostility are not always ingredients of power, neither is tolerance and acceptance, wisdom and flexibility signs of weakness. Whoever reflects and meditates on the Hudiybia will see that the Apostle overcame them by understanding, being tolerant, negotiating and out-manuvering them, be it at all time whether when he and the Muslims were in position of weakness or power.

Based on the Hudabiya wisdom, if a kaffir were to officiate an opening of a mosque, it might beneficial to the Muslims and Islam. The most important aspect of it is the acknowledgment and the public recognition of Islam and its authority. For a mosque is symbol of the presence of Islam, the heartbeat of the Muslim community, an educational outlet where the community is taught to combat evil, ignorance and apostasy. It is a university as well as a court, from where the laws of Allah are promoted, it is a symbol of authority within that community and ultimately within the state and beyond, for the Apostle of Allah said Islam rises and nothing rises above it, for it is the uppermost.

Allah who is most merciful on his slaves more they than can ever be to themselves, and because of His mercy on the Muslims, legislated rules to make it easy and lightened their burdens and eased their heavy yoke. So in Hudiybia, He legislated much that was only mercy to the Muslims of Hudiybia and the Muslims of thereafter.

The conclusion is that the events and the understanding of it teaches us victory with patience, to those who fear Allah and are devout. The thrones of those unjust will be overthrown and destroyed. The absurdity of ignorance will be vanish and the weak will be strengthened if they were to be patient. For Hudibiya teaches us to seize the opportunities to proclaim and propagate the religion of Allah. The triumph of truth over all falsehood and the defeat of the enemies of Islam, May the prayers and blessing of Allah be on our prophet Muhammad.[20]

---

[20] http://www.islameyat.com/Fatwa_26159.htm

Islam Rises Above All

Almost all Muslim scholars agree on this principle and elaborate on it in detail. Most recently Dr Abeed bin Muhammad A'Sufiyani of the University of Umm el Qurra in Mecca has researched and written extensively on the above statement. Quoting virtually every notable scholar of Islam he explains how "Islam Rises Above All" is a basic principle of the Islamic *Shari'ah* which permeates all aspects of Islamic jurisprudence. His very extensive and comprehensive research is exceedingly valuable for those who would want to understand this complex issue. However, here it would suffice to give some of his conclusions, particularly those which affect mosques and its buildings.

As a point of interest, he states Islamic directives regarding other religious buildings, especially churches: why they should not be allowed to be built, and those that need repairing and renovations must not be allowed for these are centres of *kufr* (apostasy) that spread corruption on earth, as well as are in enmity with Allah, and his Apostle.

It is accepted on the basis of the above-mentioned principle and relevant Qur'anic teaching that mosques must be higher, not only in their height, but wider and grander then all other edifices of the non-believers, in short they must be spectacular in everyway.

A mosque must be the highest and, especially in the land of the unbelievers when surrounded by unbelief, the tallest, broadest, widest in whatever other manner its superiority can be demonstrated.

This is why Muslims want the Newham mosque to be what it is portrayed, but also why in Manchester and soon in almost all major British cities the mosques will be the biggest or most spectacular buildings not only in the United Kingdom but also throughout the Western world.

Conclusion

The foregoing reflections clearly show that mosques are much more than religious outlets. Based on the Islamic views of itself and it's teaching of divisions of people in categories: Muslims and apostates, clean and profane:

Sura 9:28 *O you who have believed the pagans are profane,'*

Sura 59:20 *...not equal are the companions of the fire and the companions of the Garden, it is the companions of the garden that will achieve felicity...*

Sura 6:50 *...can the blind be held equal to the seeing? Will you then consider not?*

Sura 32:18 *Is then the man who believes no better than the man who is rebellious and wicked. Not equal are they!*

Sura 3:110 *...you (Muslims) are the best peoples evolved for mankind enjoining what is virtue and forbidding what is vice...*

Sura 4:95 *Not equal are those believers who sit and receive no hurt and those who strive and fight in the cause of Allah with their wealth and their beings, Allah has granted a grade higher to those who strive and fight with their wealth and beings than those who sit. Unto all Allah promised good but those who strive and fight hath He distinguished above those who sit by a special reward.*

The concept of the House of Peace and House of War, the self-imposed separation which is almost becoming segregation and refusal-to-assimilate and integrate, makes it divisive and discriminatory at least from the liberal democratic point of view.

Needless to say, this is not a sectarian view of the mosque, its role and function in society. It is held across the board by all schools and branches of Islam.

Finally, there is nothing at all within any Islamic movement that can be apolitical for it is defined and defines itself as a wholly encompassing system: as a socio-political, socio-religious, socio-economical, socio-legislative, judiciary, militaristic system.

Bibliography

The Noble Qur'an

Kanz Al Umal Fi sunan Al Aqwal wal Afal

Alama' Al Muttaqi Al Hindi

A'sarem Al Maslul fi Shatiem A'Rasul Shayehk Al Islam Ibn Tayymiya

Kitab Al MaGhazi Al Waqidi

Nashrat al Mujahid

Tafiseer Jame'h Albayan Fi Tafiseer Al Qur'an A'Tabari

Tafiseer Al Kashif A'Zamakhashari

Tafiseer Mafateeh Al Ghayeeb A' Tafiseer Al Kabir A'Razi

Tafiseer A'Ja' meeh Li Ahkam Al Qur'an Al Qurtabi

Tafiseer Al Qur'an Al Karim Ibn Kathir

A'sira A'Nabawiya Ibn Hashim

A'sira Al Halabiya Fi Sirat Al Amin Al Ma'mun Ali bin Burhan A'deen AlHalabi

Tarikh Al Arab Qabel Al Islam / Jawad Ali

Ahya Ulum A' Deen Imam Ghazali

Al Ahkam fi Usul Al Ahkam Ibn Hazam

Sahih Al Muslim

Sahih Al Buhkari

Nasikh wa' al Mansukh Ibn Ja'affar A' Nahass

Riyad A' Saleehin A'Dameshaqi

Nasikh Al Hadith wa Mansukhu by Al Baghdadi

Al Bidaya wa A' Nihaya by Ibn Katheer

E. J. Brill's First Encyclopaedia of Islam

Dhimmis: Jews and Christians Under Islam by Bat Ye'or

Jihad in the Cause of Allah by Abu ala Maududi

The Times newspaper

The Guardian newspaper